For Seth Pento—D.D.M.

For Dad, always my hero—J.B.H

Published by Standard Publishing, Cincinnati, Ohio

www.standardpub.com

Project editor: Robin Stanley.
Cover and interior design: Marissa Bowers.

ISBN 978-0-7847-1820-9

13 12 11 10 09 08 07   9 8 7 6 5 4 3 2

Library of Congress Cataloging-in-Publication Data

Mackall, Dandi Daley.
The armor of God / written by Dandi Daley Mackall ; pictures by Jenny B. Harris.
p. cm. -- (My favorite verses)
ISBN 0-7847-1820-2 (casebound picture book)
1. Christian life--Biblical teaching--Juvenile literature. 2. Bible. N.T. Ephesians VI, 10-18--Juvenile literature.
I. Harris, Jenny B. II. Title. III. Series: Mackall, Dandi Daley. My favorite verses.

BS2695.6.C48M33 2006   242'.62--dc22   2006000024

MY FAVORITE VERSES

I can be strong when I put on THE ARMOR OF GOD

Written by Dandi Daley Mackall   Pictures by Jenny B Harris

Standard®
PUBLISHING
Bringing The Word to Life

Cincinnati, Ohio

Sometimes the world
is a dangerous place . . .

But God keeps me safe every day.

He gives me his armor,

his sword, and his shield, and nothing can stand in my way!

A big belt of truth

is the first thing I need.
It holds up the armor I wear.
And when I remember
that God is my king,
I won't be afraid anywhere.

Stand your ground, putting on the sturdy belt of truth.

Ephesians 6:14

God sent a Savior
who died for my sin—

Now I never battle alone.

The breastplate of righteousness

covers my chest,
'cause I can't be good
on my own.

Stand your ground, putting on the...body armor of God's righteousness.

Ephesians 6:14

Jesus forgives me and loves me so much—
that's what I call real good news!

When I tell others that
God loves them, too,

I march in my
peace-loving shoes.

For shoes, put on the peace that comes from the Good News.

Ephesians 6:15

Sometimes the arrows
of doubt come my way—
somebody laughs at my hair.
That's when I hold up

my big shield
of faith,

and know and believe God is there.

In every battle you will need faith as your shield.

Ephesians 6:16

I can get worried, and I can get sad.
Crazy thoughts spin in my head.

That's when I put on

the helmet
of God

and start thinking
God's thoughts instead.

Put on salvation as your helmet.

Ephesians 6:17

If I've got a problem,
I'll look in God's Word.
I'll study the Bible each day.

It's sharp as a sword,

so it keeps me from harm
and helps me to know what to say.

Take the sword of the Spirit, which is the word of God.

Ephesians 6:17

I'll watch and I'll pray
and I'll stay on my guard,
alert when I stand, sleep, or sit.

I'm armed and protected

and ready to go.
God's armor is such
a good fit!

Pray at all times and on every occasion in the power of the Holy Spirit.

Ephesians 6:18

My life's filled with battles,
but God is my king.
He gives me his
armor and might.
I'll trust in his power,
and pray in his
name, and God
will make sure
I'm all right.

Be strong with the Lord's mighty power.

Ephesians 6:10

Ephesians 6:10-18

[10]A final word: Be strong with the Lord's mighty power.

[11]Put on all of God's armor

so that you will be able to stand firm against all strategies and tricks of the Devil. [12]For we are not fighting against people made of flesh and blood, but against the evil rulers and authorities of the unseen world, against those mighty powers of darkness who rule this world, and against wicked spirits in the heavenly realms.

¹³Use every piece of God's armor to resist the enemy in the time of evil, so that after the battle you will still be standing firm. ¹⁴Stand your ground,

Putting on the sturdy belt of truth and the body armor of God's righteousness.

¹⁵For shoes, put on the peace that comes from the Good News, so that you will be fully prepared. ¹⁶In every battle you will need faith as your shield to stop the fiery arrows aimed at you by Satan.

¹⁷Put on salvation as your helmet, and take the sword of the Spirit, which is the word of God. ¹⁸Pray at all times and on every occasion in the power of the Holy Spirit.

Stay alert and be persistent in your prayers for all Christians everywhere.